PUT THE OVEN ON

TRISH TAYLOR

For the Lingards —

In gratitude for your friendship, generous hospitality,

and wonderful food.

Contents

Put the Oven On: An American's Guide to British Food, And Why It's Not as Bad as You Think

by

Trish Taylor

Copyright © October 2022 by Trish Taylor

The moral right of the author has been asserted.

www.trishtaylorauthor.com

Credits
Book Cover Design
Vanessa Mendozzi

Copy Editing
Positively Proofed
info@positivelyproofed.com

ISBN: 978-1-7328655-7-0

Introduction

I imagine you're here because of your curiosity about the food of the British Isles. Or you might live abroad and are nostalgic about the biscuits and snacks, or you miss the chocolate and long for a decent cup of tea. Or maybe you're planning to visit the UK and are not sure what to order in a pub or restaurant. Whatever the reason, I hope you'll find inspiration to seek out the food of Britain and even make some in your own kitchen.

When I first moved to the US, I wandered around supermarkets searching in vain for food items, because I didn't know the American name. Self-checkout was frustrating for the same reason. When is a courgette not a courgette? When it's a zucchini, of course. This guide will help you find what you are looking for without having to accost strangers.

There are unique options and variations in the different countries of the United Kingdom. Scotland, Wales, and Northern Ireland have their own delights. I've mainly focused on the foods of England, only because that's where I'm from, and where I have done most of my eating and shopping. Where food is specific to the other countries and areas of the UK, I will indicate with:

(S) Scotland

(W) Wales

(I) Northern Ireland

(N) The North of England

To save you time searching, you may find that some information appears in more than one chapter. If you need a definition of food or related terms, you will find it in the list at the back.

This book was inspired by an outpouring of interest in the food-related chapters of my book, *Put the Kettle On: An American's Guide to British Slang, Telly and Tea*. A small amount of that material was rewritten and updated to be included here.

I don't know where you might visit in the UK. I've therefore focused on foods that are readily available and common to many locations. In towns and villages, you will find farmers markets, wineries where you can sample wines and ciders, and creameries with amazing cheeses. You may also find Christmas outdoor markets selling unique food and crafts.

I want to point you toward food that people tell me they've enjoyed when visiting the UK. This is only a glimpse into the food and drink traditions of Great Britain. The information is sourced from the best of my knowledge and according to my research, which was correct at the time of writing.

Where Did the Bad British Food Idea Come From?

We begin with the stereotype about bad British food. We'll get it out of the way before we dive into all the food that Brits enjoy. When I meet people who delight in telling me how terrible British food is, the common theme is that either they've never visited the United Kingdom or they have limited experience with British food. There is also no accounting for taste. I find the idea of sweet potatoes cooked with sugar and marshmallows the least-appetizing side dish imaginable. My American husband feels the same way about beans on toast. Some Americans may find British food bland as it has less salt added than what they are used to.

Admittedly, there are Brits who prefer their food without seasoning, or those who believe that the only role of garlic is to ward off vampires. You'll discover that the reality differs from what you've been led to believe, especially when you learn about how much curry and spicy food Brits eat.

Another belief is that Brits overcook their vegetables until they are nothing but mush. This might have been true in some households decades ago. Nowadays, Brits know how to cook *al dente.* If you're going to come after us for overcooking our veggies, I will have to mention that vegetables in the US often come over-salted and mixed with bits of meat and sometimes laced with cream and meat stock. Maybe our vegetables are just a little more understated —like us.

Seriously, British food is different, not better or worse, and being prepared to adapt your palate will help you enjoy the experience. Full disclosure: I grew up in a household that overcooked our veggies. The joke was that we put the vegetables on the stove in October, to be sure they would be ready for Christmas dinner. I would guess that if you visit the UK, you are unlikely to eat mushy vegetables cooked by someone's grandma. Every home has its food idiosyncrasies. Our dad would pour the cooling tea from his pint pot onto his cornflakes instead of milk. I have other family members who can happily eat a pork pie between two slices of bread.

The terrible food narrative owes much to stories told by United States servicemen and women stationed in the UK during World War II. They returned home with tales of unappetizing food and limited culinary choices. While American G.I.s were busy wooing British women with silk stockings and chocolate, they were also storing up their accounts of gristly meat and boiled cabbage. Much of the food wasn't great, partly because of rationing. There was a war on, after all. Rationing of goods, including food, started in 1940 and continued until 1954. Everyone, including children, was issued a ration book and could only buy food if they had enough rations. The government adapted the amounts allowed, depending on personal circumstances— pregnant women, those with diabetes, and medical conditions were given exceptions—and the changing situation as the war progressed. Rationing made it a challenge to cook tasty meals because of the limited availability of many ingredients.

Some studies have claimed that Brits were healthier during rationing as unhealthy foods were limited. Individuals had only a few ounces of dairy and meat per week, with similar restrictions on sugar. Some foods were simply not available or in short supply because of the war. Many children never saw a banana while growing up. Vegetables, however, were not rationed. The government even encouraged citizens to grow their own. They needed no ration coupon for offal.

This reality offers another clue as to the origin of the awful food myth. Cooks learned to be creative with their recipes. Dishes such as steak and kidney pie and liver and onions became common. The government's Ministry of Food also created recipes that encouraged British households to cook meals that included the most widely available foods. Though top chefs now serve offal as a delicacy in exclusive restaurants, Americans during wartime were apparently not impressed.

Britain no longer has rationing, nor food shortages, and meat is not limited to offal. It's time we all push negative stories about Britain's food out of our minds. Be open to a culinary adventure and let me guide you in the right direction.

This book isn't about gourmet food but rather what to look for when eating at restaurants that suit most visitors' budgets, or shopping for groceries or treats to take back home. It's also not a recipe book, yet if you want to try your hand at British baking, I will introduce you to what you'll need in your store cupboard.

We'll explore what Brits eat, from food in tins and packets to the freezer section of the supermarket. Because many do. We'll look at what you might find on an average buffet. Yes, they can be somewhat beige. Hey, we like our pies and pasties. And we'll contemplate curry, which you might say isn't British, though the Indian food that Brits eat is often a hybrid created to suit the British palate. It's what Brits eat, and that's what we are here to talk about.

If you look for poor quality and tasteless food, you can find it. You can also find fabulous food. I recommend that if you visit, talk to the locals, buy a guidebook, or look on review sites and online guides. Don't let a lack of understanding and prejudice stop you from enjoying some wonderful food, often at a very reasonable price.

Vegan and Vegetarian

The UK has lots of options if you're looking for meals that don't include meat or animal products. Whether a vegan option in a restaurant, a vegetarian topping for a baked potato in a cafe, vegan, or ready meals in the supermarket, you'll be spoiled for choice. Pub meals usually have a range of vegetarian and vegan options, too.

Other Special Dietary Requirements

Most food establishments will also offer gluten-free, low carb, or any dietary options that you may require.

Food standards and additives

Compared to American items, you'll find a difference in the ingredients of British packaged foods. Foods are required to be labeled if they include additives that may be harmful to children. Known as "e" numbers in the UK, the food additives in children's foods are mostly related to food coloring, which many manufacturers have replaced with safer alternatives. You might also find that food goes off (expires) more quickly because some food has fewer or no preservatives.

Portion sizes in restaurants

Though portion sizes are often smaller in the UK than what you are used to, it depends on what type of restaurant you are eating in. On my last visit, I found fish-and-chip portions to be huge.

Dinner Invites

If a Brit invites you to dine with them, make sure you're clear what time of day you will be eating. In the North of England, many people still refer to their lunchtime meal as dinner. If you're invited to come for tea, they might mean an evening meal rather than a cup of tea.

Bearing in mind that this book is about food in Britain, I don't want you to get confused. So while you're reading, just pretend you are in the UK. We'll be calling "chips" the things you eat with fish, and "crisps" are what you call "chips." Okay, now we've got that out of the way. Let's go start with breakfast.

ONE

Breakfast

Full English Breakfast/Fry-up

A full English, also known as a *fry-up*, is a splendid way to start the day. It's often a weekend treat or enjoyed when on holiday (vacation). You can find variations of a Full English served in pubs and cafes. You can also usually find vegetarian substitutions for the meat products. Expect to find bacon, sausage, mushrooms, eggs, fried bread, tinned (canned) tomatoes, baked beans, black pudding (N), toast, and tea or coffee.

Across the border in Scotland, you may find the addition of a square sausage known as a Lorne Sausage, Tattie (potato) scones, oatcakes, porridge, or kippers.

In Wales, look for traditional laverbread made from edible seaweed.

An Irish breakfast may have the addition of potatoes or hash browns and potato bread, or soda bread. In Northern Ireland, it's known as an *Ulster fry*.

If you're enjoying your Full English in a British café in Spain or other popular European destinations, they might serve you chips alongside the other traditional fry-up items. Yes, Brits are guilty of traveling to far-off lands and eating exactly the same food that they enjoy at home.

Continental Breakfast

There was a time when some establishments served a croissant and a glass of orange juice and called it *Continental*. Many places now offer the real deal, with the type of breakfast food you might enjoy in France or Germany: platters of meat, cheese, pastries, and fruit.

Toast

Toast is a popular mainstay of British breakfasts. Stay in a bed-and-breakfast or a hotel and you'll often be served a little toast rack with your choice of white or brown toast. If you stay in a hotel in Spain—or any other British tourist hotspots—you'll more likely serve yourself using the conveyer-belt toasters you get in some hotels in the US.

Bacon Sandwich/Butty

Most Brits will drool at the thought of a bacon sandwich, which is an iconic breakfast food. British bacon is not normally the streaky kind, though you can find it if that's your preference. Bacon rashers are a lean slice of meat with fat at the edge, rather than streaks of fat running through it, and come smoked or unsmoked. The bread that makes up the sandwich is a buttered, soft, white bread roll or sliced white bread. The favored condiment is brown sauce or tomato ketchup. You might prefer it without sauce, though if you ask for mayonnaise, expect to be run out of town. A bacon sandwich is also a popular hangover food—I didn't say "cure."

· · ·

Black Pudding: Sausage made from pork or beef blood, blended with cereal and suet. Yup, blood pudding. This book is not an endorsement of all foods. You may also see white pudding on a breakfast menu, which is similar but has meat products that replace the blood.

Crumpets: Like an English muffin, with a softer consistency. The original and best way to eat them is to toast until light golden brown and then spread with enough butter so that it melts and seeps through the holes onto your plate. Some enjoy crumpets topped with cheese, or even baked beans. To each their own, I guess.

Eggs with soldiers: Soft-boiled eggs with sliced strips of bread or toast, which are often referred to as "soldiers." Though normally served to young children, if you like runny eggs and comfort food, this is for you. You will need to root around the back of the cupboard for your eggcups.

Eggy bread: French toast. Eggy bread is a simpler affair than American-style French toast. We rarely serve it with icing (powdered) sugar or maple syrup. You must admit, syrup on eggs is odd.

Fried bread: Sliced bread fried in lard or butter and crisped to perfection. This is the food your doctor tells you not to eat.

4

Kedgeree: Curry-flavored rice, smoked haddock, and eggs. You're unlikely to be served kedgeree in a mid-range hotel or bed-and-breakfast. It's a posh dish that the upper-class eat for breakfast.

Kippers: Smoked herrings

Marmalade on toast: A slightly bitter orange preserve spread on toast. Lime marmalade also is available and simply fabulous.

Pikelets: Similar to crumpets, but thinner and wider.

Porridge: Oatmeal

Welsh rarebit: Fancy cheese on toast. A thick cheese topping with a runny consistency made with spices and beer. Served over toast. Don't let the word "runny" put you off. Cooked properly, it's delicious.

TWO

Eating Out

Restaurants

Eating out in the United Kingdom is a more leisurely affair than in the US. Brits eat out less frequently; it's more of an occasion. Since moving to the US, I've noticed that many of my friends and coworkers eat out multiple times a week, often for the convenience of not having to cook or go grocery shopping, rather than as a social occasion. In the UK, it is not uncommon to enjoy a three-course meal spaced out over as many hours. In the US, I've rarely spent more than a couple of hours over a meal. Busy restaurants are often keen to clear the table to ready for the next sitting. In the UK, you may need to reserve a table in advance, though once you have a reservation, it's often yours for the evening. You also won't get staff bugging you every five minutes to check if you're enjoying your meal. Maybe it's because the wait staff aren't relying on you for tips, and they know most Brits don't feel comfortable being interrupted so frequently. This is different in big cities or in restaurants that are in high demand. Brits also eat out later. When planning to eat at a restaurant, check their opening times. Some don't open on Mondays, though this is more often in smaller towns and villages.

Afternoon Tea

Afternoon tea (sometimes called High Tea) is a treat many Americans enjoy when visiting the UK. Do your research to avoid paying over the odds (overpaying) for a lackluster menu. There are fancy offerings at some of the top restaurants in big cities, or you might find a perfectly delightful tea at a country tearoom or hotel. The meal comprises a selection of small sandwiches, cakes, and pastries, and often scones with jam and cream, and tea, of course. You can also often upgrade to include wine or champagne. It can be a pleasant way to while away an afternoon or mark a celebration. Be mindful, there is often a lot of bread, pastry, and cake to be eaten in a short period.

Mini Picnic Bench Afternoon Tea

A modern twist to afternoon tea is the *Picnic Bench* version instead of traditional fare. More contemporary options are served on a mini picnic bench rather than the three-tier stand. Foods that Americans may recognize include mini burgers and milk shakes, as well as other fare you wouldn't expect at afternoon tea, such as fish and chips.

Cream Tea

Although originating from Devon and Cornwall, traditional cream teas are widely available in cafes and restaurants. A cream tea comprises a scone, which is split in the middle and spread with fresh-clotted cream and jam, with a pot of tea or coffee. There is an ongoing debate about whether you should put cream or jam on first. You'll usually be served the cream and jam separately, so you can decide for yourself. If you can get the cream to go on first without the jam sliding off into your lap, good luck to you.

The Carvery

If you want to experience a traditional roast dinner but haven't convinced a Brit family to feed you, a carvery is a suitable alternative. Often found attached to pubs and hotels, this dining experience is like an American buffet and features various roasted meats. The diner chooses their meat, which is then carved for them as they line up with their plate. The meal includes a choice of side dishes and traditional puddings and desserts. Please note that carveries are not "eat all you can" buffets. You're not usually allowed to go back for another helping. If you see a Brit balancing a plate brimming with food they can barely carry, they are just getting their money's worth.

High-end Restaurants

There are top-quality restaurants in big cities and small villages. Whether you are looking for a restaurant with a Michelin star or food from a celebrity chef, you will have plenty of choices if you have the funds. If you're an adventurous carnivore, you may get to sample wild game. Game is strong-tasting meat from hunted birds and other animals. This might include duck, grouse, hare, partridge, pigeon, quail, or venison. Be aware that there is strong environmental and ethical opposition to game, and some restaurants have taken it off their menu.

British restaurants also offer fish that is not fried in batter. This might include Dover sole, halibut, turbot, and monkfish.

Weekend editions of quality newspapers have eating-out guides with features and reviews on top restaurants. Be aware that some food, such as game, is seasonal.

Gratuities/Tipping

Tipping, though not an automatic expectation in restaurants in the UK, is becoming more of an accepted custom. (Bloody Americans, taking our women and now making us tip.) Servers are paid at least the minimum wage; customers are not expected to make up their wages in tips. You may see service charges in big cities. High-end restaurants may add a gratuity—sometimes between 10% and 12.5%. Tips, of course, are always appreciated. Brits didn't always tip bar staff. Times are changing, and a 10% service charge might be added at bars. In pubs, it is customary to offer the bar person a drink, who may then agree to "have one later" and take a tip in the amount equal to a drink.

Pizza

Be open to unique toppings in British pizza restaurants and takeaways. Yes, we really do put fish on our pizzas.

Popular toppings include:

Tuna and sweetcorn

Ham and pineapple

Seafood pizza—May include prawn and tuna.

Keema pizza—In areas of the UK where pizzas are sold in Indian takeaways (to-go), you might also have curry on top of your pizza.

Meal Deals and Pasties

Work lunches differ in the UK from those in the US. Many of my American friends regularly eat out at lunchtime. In the UK, it's more of a treat than a daily occurrence. An option for those who don't make their own sandwiches for lunch is the *meal deal.*

High-street (main-street) stores offer great value deals. The meal deal comprises of a sandwich or wrap, a snack such as crisps or granola bars, plus a drink. Individual items can add up to almost three times the deal price, which at the time of writing is often between £3.00 and £5.00. Even if you don't go for the meal deal, you can also find sandwiches in high-street stores for a bargain price. If you get hungry waiting for your plane at the airport, the high-street stores that sell meal deals also offer some of the same items in their airport stores. Bakery chains are another good option for lunches or snacks while shopping, and they also offer meal deals. A breakfast of a bacon sandwich and a coffee are priced from £2.00, or lunch from £3.00. Where can you get that kind of deal in the US? Coffee chains also sell sandwiches, bakery items, and the full range of coffees and beverages. And yes, they do iced coffee, too. Expect to pay higher prices for the more upmarket coffees and premium sandwiches and toasties.

Food at the Cinema (Movies)

There are some variations between British cinema food and that found in US movie theaters. Many Brits prefer sweet popcorn. It was once the only kind available. You can also get salted popcorn and mixed options: sweet and salty, and concoctions drizzled with chocolate and caramel. Other foods you may see in the US that are available at British cinemas include hotdogs, chips and salsa, and nachos. They also serve ice cream, wine, and beer. In upmarket cinemas, you can find a wine and champagne list, plus chai tea, smoothies, sharing plates, and even garlic bread, although I'm not sure I want the stranger next to me eating pungent food.

Early Bird Specials

Many restaurants offer special deals for those who want to eat out early and get home in time for their favorite soap opera. You may find special-priced menus offering a two- or three-course meal.

In big cities, you'll find food from all over the world. "'But it's not British,' you say!" Everything came from somewhere. The United Kingdom is culturally richer for its diversity, and that is especially true for its food—whether you enjoy the scrummiest fish and chips, the tastiest curry, or the most delicious cream tea. I hope you find eating out a wonderful experience.

THREE

Fish and Chips

The Chippy: The fish-and-chip shop

Fish and chips continue to be a popular takeaway meal in the UK. Though there may not be quite as many fish-and-chip shops as there once were, good chippies still can draw long queues, especially on a Friday. Friday has long been the most popular day to eat fish and chips. It harks back to times when many Christians abstained from eating meat on Fridays during Lent. Now it's a Friday tradition, no matter your beliefs.

Fish and chips: A piece of cod or haddock coated in batter and deep-fried, accompanied by chips (fries). Though traditional fish-and-chip shops use beef dripping for frying, vegetable oil is now widely available.

Fish and chips are still often served wrapped in paper, though not in an old newspaper as was the tradition before health and safety concerns came along.

Buttered teacake: A large, soft, buttered bread roll.

Chip butty: Chips, in a buttered teacake. (N)

Fish butty: A portion of fish in a buttered teacake. (N)

Fishcake: A potato-and-fish patty coated in batter and fried. (N)

In other parts of the country, they might cook a fishcake in breadcrumbs, and with different fish such as salmon.

Battered sausage: A large, battered-and-fried sausage link.

Saveloy sausage: A highly seasoned red sausage. You are more likely to see this in the South of England.

Scraps/bits: The bits of batter that fall off the fish as it fries. The fryer sieves them from the hot oil and deposits them in the warmer, alongside the cooked fish.

As kids, we'd go to the chippy and buy a bag of chips to share. The familiar refrain, "A bag of chips with scraps on, please" is likely still heard today, especially in the North of England.

You may also find:

Mushy peas

Gravy

Onion rings

Curry sauce

Pickled onions

And always—salt and malt vinegar.

The Special

A *special* can mean different things, depending on where you are. In Scotland and other parts of the UK, it's fish coated in breadcrumbs rather than batter. In other areas, as was my experience in Yorkshire, it's an extra-large fish that must be specially ordered when entering the chippy.

Scottish Fish-and-Chip Shops

Chippies in Scotland are renowned for offering unique battered and deep-fried items, including chocolate bars and crème eggs. You might have seen similar novelties like deep-fried cookies at state fairs in the US. Don't expect to find these items in every establishment. The potential for tainting the oil used for frying fish and chips means that not every owner will be prepared to satisfy your late-night urge for deep-fried chocolate in batter. Most of the deep-fried items you will find will be savory. These include *Pizza Crunch*, a slice of pizza deep-fried in batter, or you might have a craving for deep-fried black pudding.

Skin

It's a contentious issue. Should we eat fish cooked with the skin left on? This argument often falls on a North/South divide. Northerners rarely do skin, no matter how much top chefs tell us it's full of nutrients. We don't *expect* fish and chips to be good for us.

Fish-and-chip Restaurants

Sit-down restaurants are a popular venue for a family dinner where they offer full table service. Expect different styles and sizes of fish to suit all appetites. They usually have traditional puddings, too. Order bread and butter so you can make your own chip butty.

FOUR

Curry/Indian Food

So popular is curry in Britain, some have claimed it as an unofficial national dish. From chain pubs and high-end restaurants to bargain-priced takeaways serving curry alongside fish and chips, kebabs, and pizzas, curry is available almost everywhere. You'll find an abundance of takeaway and restaurant choices with Indian, Pakistani, or Bengali food.

In cities with diverse populations, you can also find international stores selling all the spices you'd need should you want to make your own food. Many supermarkets also have international or world food aisles offering an abundance of spices. Pre-made curry sauces in jars are widely available. Add them to your choice of meat, fish, or vegetables for a quick and easy way to make curry.

British supermarkets sell ready-made curries, starters, and accompaniments, including brands from top Indian restaurants. You can fill your fridge with samosa, pakoras, and bhajis to have Indian snacks whenever you want.

Brits refer to those from India, Pakistan, and anywhere in Southeast Asia as *Asian*. I am using the term "Indian" to refer to the type of restaurants, as that's how they often market themselves. The proprietors or management may not be Indian. Food served in Indian restaurants may not be "traditional" in the sense that it may differ from what they cook in Indian households. Restaurants cater to British tastebuds. It is, however, different to what's served in the US, where I've found it necessary to request my food *Indian hot* if I want it to resemble what I'm used to in the UK. A too-hot curry can lead people to swear off trying it again. If you're not sure how hot you'd like it, start with a mild heat level, and ask for recommendations. If you're new to the wonders of Indian food, give it a chance. I can almost guarantee that you will be hooked; it is a little addictive.

What to Order in an Indian Restaurant

If you are unsure what to order in Indian restaurants, here are some popular dishes with brief descriptions. Check to see if main courses/entrees come with rice or other additions before ordering extra.

Starters/Accompaniments

Aloo chaat: Hot, spicy snack of cubed potatoes that are boiled before frying.

Chana chaat: Potatoes and chickpea salad in a tamarind sauce.

Chapatis: Thin, round, whole-wheat flatbread. You need this (or a naan) to scoop up that delicious curry.

Chutney: Cooling or spicy relishes often served with poppadoms.

Naan bread: Fluffy flatbread cooked with yoghurt and baked in a clay oven. Try it plain or with garlic, cheese, or stuffed with various fillings.

Onion bhajis: Deep-fried onions coated in a batter made with gram flour (ground chickpeas).

Pakora: Deep-fried spicy fish, meat, or vegetable fritters.

Pilau rice: Spicy cooked rice with vegetables.

Poppadoms: Round, thin, spicy, fried crisp bread.

Raita: Yoghurt-based dip with mint spices and cucumber.

Samosas: Triangles of deep-fried savory pastry filled with vegetables or meat.

Vegetable pakora: Deep-fried spicy vegetable fritter.

Curries

Aloo gobi: Potato and cauliflower curry

Balti: A type of curry cooked and served in an iron balti pan.

Bhuna: A dry curry. Usually with a choice of prawn, vegetable, chicken, or other meats.

Biryani: Rice-based curry

Chana masala: Lentil curry

Chicken tikka masala: Roasted chicken dish, cooked in spices. It is so popular that some claim it as one of Britain's national dishes.

Dhal: Lentil-based curry

Keema: Minced (ground), meat-based curry.

Mutter paneer: Indian cheese and peas.

Tandoori chicken: Chicken dish cooked in a clay oven.

Thali: A platter of various small dishes.

Vegetable sabzi: Mixed vegetables

Vindaloo: A very hot curry. Order at your own risk.

Tindaloo: Even hotter!

Desserts

Gajar Halwa: Carrot-based dessert

Gulab Jamun: Fried curd dumplings with pistachio, served with syrup.

Kulfi: Traditional ice cream

Mango lassi: Yoghurt-based drink

As well as finding desserts in Indian restaurants, Asian dessert restaurants and sweet parlors also are becoming popular in bigger cities.

FIVE

Pubs and Drinking Culture

Watch British TV and you might believe that Brits spend every night in their local pub. Though the availability of inexpensive alcohol from supermarkets has contributed to many pubs closing their doors, you can still find excellent food and warm hospitality in pubs, especially in destination and country pubs. Chain pubs offering cheap drinks and even cheaper food have also replaced some local pubs.

The legal drinking age in the UK is eighteen. Children are allowed in pubs with beer gardens. Those sixteen and over are allowed in pubs if accompanied by an adult and not consuming alcohol—at the bar owner's discretion.

It's not unusual for young people to be given alcohol at home. You cannot legally give alcohol to children under five. Otherwise, it's the parents' decision. The attitude toward drinking in the UK is fairly relaxed, except when it comes to drink-driving, which has serious penalties. Public transportation, taxis, and ride-booking services are widely available in most places, so there's really no excuse. In the US, you need to go to a liquor store to buy spirits (hard liquor). In most of the UK, you can get any type of alcohol in any place that has a license. This could be a supermarket, local store, or hotel.

The Myth About Warm Beer

Before we begin, we must dispense with another stereotype/heresy spoken of British traditions— that of Brits drinking warm beer. If you order lager—blonde/light-colored beer—they will serve it ice cold as you have it back home. *Real ale*, or dark beers, are not chilled but served at the temperature of the cellar, a tad cooler than room temperature. This is deliberate to allow the imbiber to taste the beer rather than freeze out the subtle flavor.

Alcoholic Drinks

Liqueurs

In the UK, a liqueur (pronounced li'kyoor) is different than liquor. It is a distilled drink, normally sweet and infused with herbs and possibly fruit. If offered a liqueur after dinner, it may be a glass of port or similar rich alcoholic drink. What Americans call "liquor stores" are known in the UK as "off-licenses."

Drinks in UK pubs and bars

Advocaat: An alcoholic eggnog

Bitter: Dark beer

Brut: Dry sparkling wine

Cava: Spanish sparkling wine. A popular alternative to champagne.

Cider: British cider is always an alcoholic drink, unless you specify a desire for a non-alcoholic version. There are now many options besides apple cider, including summer fruits, tropical, and even rhubarb and custard.

Gin: A gin and tonic was once the only way to drink gin. You can now find gin of every flavor. Gin bars are a huge trend, serving a wide range of craft gins flavored with herbs, spices, and exotic additives.

Ginger wine: Fortified ginger drink, sipped with or without ice or added to Scotch whisky to make a whisky mac.

Ice and a slice: Ice and a slice of fresh lemon. Ice is a cube or two. Don't expect to be given half a glass full.

Lager: Light-colored or blonde beer, sometimes served with lime or black currant cordial.

Mild: Traditional dark ale with a lower alcohol content than bitter.

Pimm's: A gin-based fruit cup that is popular in the summer. Drank as a cocktail with fruit and lemonade. Popular at Wimbledon.

Port: Fortified wine

Prosecco: Italian sparkling wine

Shandy: Lemonade mixed with beer

Shandy top: A splash of lemonade in your beer

Stout: Strong dark beer

Short: Distilled drink or liquor. If someone offers to buy you a short with your drink, that's a shot of liquor—whisky, brandy, etc. Also known as a chaser.

Snakebite: Half lager and half cider in a pint glass. Drink too many and you'll understand why it is so named.

Snowball: A mixture of advocaat, lemonade, and a splash of lime juice. Mixed to make it frothy. Popular with the older generation, or some may have it as a festive treat.

Sweet sherry: Fortified wine

Pop (Soda) and Soft Drinks

If you're having a soft drink or soda with your meal, remember, refills are rarely offered. Also, you may have to ask for ice. Pubs serve a wide range of soft drinks. There is also an amazing choice of alcohol-free beers, wines, ciders, and even non-alcoholic distilled spirits in bars and restaurants, and also available in supermarkets and off-licenses.

Cream soda: Traditional sweet soda with vanilla flavor.

Dandelion and burdock: Old-style, dark-colored soda with a unique flavor.

Elderflower: A uniquely British flavor. Look for a variety of combinations available, such as apple and elderflower or elderflower and raspberry.

Lemonade: Clear, soda-type drink similar to 7UP. (What Americans call "lemonade" is called "cloudy" or "traditional" lemonade.) We use lemonade as a mixer with beer and shots, as well as served on its own to children.

Lime and soda: A shot of sweet lime cordial topped up with on-tap soda water.

Water: Servers in food establishments will not automatically bring water to the table. If you ask for water, clarify whether you want tap water, or they may serve you premium and costly bottled or mineral water.

Instant vs. 'Proper' Coffee

Many Brits—it's hard to get up-to-date figures, but probably over 50%—drink instant coffee at home. Millennial Brits are drinking more ground/fresh coffee, referred to as *proper* coffee, so this will probably eventually change. Though Brits enjoy proper coffee when someone else is making it, or in coffee bars and restaurants, they just can't be bothered making it themselves and enjoy the convenience of instant. The UK has an excellent range of good-quality instant coffee available.

Types of Pubs

The local: Often a small, simple pub where everyone knows each other.

Bar and restaurant/bar and bistro: More upmarket option

Chain pubs: Offer inexpensive drinks and food; some are top end and expensive.

Gastro pubs: Upmarket (more upscale) dining

Country pubs: Usually in scenic spots with seating outside and an excellent selection of food and beer.

Micropubs: Small, independent establishments offering craft beers.

Wine Bars and Cocktail Bars

If you're looking for nightlife in town centers, you are more likely to find wine and cocktail bars than pubs. Rather than beers on tap, you will find bottled beer, wine, champagne, and cocktails. Brits are going upmarket!

Pub Food

Pub food has come a long way from the pie and a pint, though they still offer traditional fare.

Popular offerings include:

Crusty sandwiches/baguettes

There's nothing better than a doorstep sandwich: big, thick hunks of bread with your choice of filling or a stuffed French baguette or crusty bread.

Pickled eggs

You may see this unusual delicacy atop the bar in the local pub—boiled eggs swimming in a huge jar, pickled in vinegar or brine.

Pie and peas

Hot pie with savory fillings, which could include steak and kidney, pork, or a vegetarian option. Green peas are "steeped" overnight with water and bicarbonate of soda (baking soda), then boiled to make a mushy paste. Mushy peas are another misunderstood food item. They may not look appetizing yet taste good with pies and mint sauce.

Ploughman's (Plowman's) lunch

Although a "Ploughman's" was originally a simple meal that the ploughman could take into the field and eat cold between ploughing, it has evolved into a much fancier affair at some pubs. Usually a combination of thick, crusty bread, a hunk of cheese, often with ham, or a slice of meat pie, an apple, and pickle—the brown, crunchy type.

Sunday roast

The Sunday dinner or Sunday roast is a beloved tradition among Brits. Served both in the home and in pubs and restaurants. A traditional roast —usually roast beef with roast potatoes, Yorkshire puddings, and vegetables. If you're lucky, a traditional sweet pudding may follow lunch.

Yorkshire pudding

Yorkshire pudding is a small, puffed-up, savory pudding made from pancake mixture. It's similar to a popover and normally eaten with a roast dinner. Pubs often sell large, plate-size Yorkshire puddings. They're filled with savory brown gravy and possibly meat and vegetables.

Other Pub Menu Items

Bangers and mash: Sausage and mashed potatoes

Burgers and chips: Brits enjoy burgers, too, and many pubs offer fancy toppings and variations.

Fat chips: Fries, cut extra-large

Fish and chips: Fish and French fries

Halloumi/Halloumi fries: This tasty Cypriot grilling cheese is a hugely popular menu item. There are also local versions available.

Gammon and chips: Thick-sliced ham with fries. Sometimes topped with pineapple.

Jacket potato: Baked potato, served with a choice of toppings.

Lancashire hotpot: A stew topped with sliced potatoes

Scampi and chips: Fried shrimp in breadcrumbs

Scotch egg: Hard-boiled eggs, wrapped in sausage meat, coated in breadcrumbs, and fried.

Shepherd's pie: Savory mashed-potato-topped pie with a ground meat base. Traditionally, Shepherd's pie uses lamb; cottage pie uses beef.

Toad in the hole: Sausages cooked in Yorkshire pudding.

Welsh rarebit: Fancy toasted cheese that's often cooked in beer.

Getting a Round In

When drinking in a group, it's customary to take turns ordering and paying for drinks. This is "getting a round in" or "standing a round." After someone has bought a round, the next person volunteers. If there is a sizable group, it can be expensive. If you don't want to join a round because of cost, or if you're only drinking soft drinks, you can declare, "I'll get my own. I'm only having one. I'm driving," or whatever reason you don't want to be in the round. Whatever you do, don't join a round and then not stand (pay for) your round. It's simply not British, neither is going to the loo just as the drinks are about to be ordered to avoid paying. It's also impolite to order excessively expensive drinks when it's someone else's round. When buying a round it's also common to buy a selection of crisps, place the bags on the table, and split open for everyone to share. Your drinking buddies may believe you are one of those rich Americans they've seen on TV. If you indeed do have deep pockets, you can declare, "Drinks all round." Be careful. This could cost you more than your flight home.

Last Orders

Licensing laws have changed over the past two decades, and "last orders" is not what it was. Traditionally near closing time, the publican/pub owner would call "last orders," which was your last chance to get a drink. At closing time, they called "time." After that, you were in "drinking-up time," a window of time to finish your drink.

Nowadays, pubs don't have the same strict rules and can serve drinks within their license whenever they want. A landlord or landlady of the pub can still tell you to drink up when they've decided it's time to close. If you're friends with the owners, you might get invited to a *lock in* as their guest. You cannot legally buy drinks outside of licensing hours, but they can give them to you for free. This was a more common practice when opening hours were shorter.

Shared Tables

When eating in pubs, you usually order at the bar, and the food is brought to your table. If it's busy, you may not get a table to yourself. It's polite to ask if it's OK to share a stranger's table, and most people will not refuse. I mean we're British, the awkwardness of risking a confrontation by saying no to a stranger is almost as bad as having to share a table with them. In fancier places, they may do table service in a separate dining area.

SIX

Bread and Sandwiches

Bread

Britain has many tasty bread options. Bread buns and loaves have a multitude of different names, depending on where you are in the United Kingdom. A bread bun/roll could be referred to as any of the following. I have given descriptions for those that differ from a simple bread roll.

· · ·

Bap: Scottish soft bread roll

Barm cake: Northwest England name for a bread roll.

Brioche rolls: Rich bread rolls baked with eggs and butter.

Flatcake: An extra-large teacake

Morning roll: Simple bread roll

Stotty cake: Heavy, large flatcake from the Northeast of England.

Teacake: Not to be confused with the chocolate-covered marshmallow with a biscuit base and a jammy middle. A teacake that is used to make a sandwich differs from the type used for a toasted teacake, which should have raisins or sultanas.

Other Types of Bread and Bread Products

Baguette: French breadstick

Bara brith: Welsh tea bread

Bloomer: Large, oval-shaped, crusty bread loaf

Crusty bread: Usually a large white loaf with a fluffy interior and crusty outside.

Crusty cob: Round, crusty bread loaf

Danish: Sliced white bread, often lighter and smaller than regular loaves.

Farmhouse loaf: Traditional-style bread, baked in a rectangular tin.

Finger roll: Hotdog bun

Fruit loaf: Sweet, dense tea bread made with dried fruit.

Granary: Wholemeal bread with grains and seeds.

Hot cross buns: Sweet fruit bread roll, decorated with an iced cross. Eaten during the period leading up to Easter. Some stores have them available all year round. They are also available with fancy options in posh shops. Salted caramel hot cross bun, anyone?

Iced finger: A finger roll topped with icing. Iced bread (sounds weird), though you will be surprised how good it tastes.

Malt Loaf: Dense and chewy fruit bread, usually spread with butter.

Sally Lunn: A large, sweet bun/teacake originating from Bath.

Scotch pancakes: Small, sweet pancake often served cold with butter.

Tiger bread: Large, crusty loaf, baked with a glaze that creates a mottled pattern on the crusty surface to resemble an animal print.

Toastie bread: Bread especially made for toasting.

Wholemeal: Whole wheat

Sandwiches

Sandwiches, sarnies, or butties are the staple of the British lunch. Sold in cafes and supermarkets, or taken in your packed lunch, and eaten in a vast array of bread choices. Brits can make a sandwich out of anything.

Bacon sarnie/butty: The king of breakfast sandwiches; rashers of bacon in buttered bread. See Breakfast chapter for more on bacon.

Chip sandwich/butty: Chips (fries) in buttered bread

Crisp sandwiches: These have become a cult classic. Brits put what you call "chips" between buttered bread or a buttered teacake. A student/drunk habit now conjures nostalgia. Everyone remembers where they were when they were eating a diet of crisp sandwiches. Crisp manufacturers have also latched onto the idea and use it in their marketing.

Fish finger (fish stick) sandwich: Once a speedy snack or served as a children's meal. It's now an almost acceptable meal for grownups. They serve its upmarket cousin in restaurants and pubs. The frozen version, replaced with a menu item such as Chef's creation of freshly caught goujons of cod, served between granary bread and a crisp rocket salad with a homemade tartare (tartar) sauce. Sounds lovely, but there's nothing wrong with four fish fingers between two slices of buttered white bread.

Egg mayonnaise/egg and cress: Egg salad, usually with a sprinkling of watercress.

Egg sandwich/butty: Fried egg sandwich

Salad sandwich: A sandwich so common in the UK that I was surprised to discover how an American friend was confused at my craving for a salad sandwich. "What kind of salad would I have in this imagined sandwich?" she inquired. The misunderstanding makes sense when you realize that in the US, egg mayonnaise is called egg salad, tuna mayo is tuna salad, etc.

When ordering a sandwich in the US, the first consideration is the desired meat or protein; the salad is an addition. In the UK, the salad *is* the sandwich, with meat or cheese added. Are you still wondering what kind of salad? We rarely refer to a dish as salad unless it includes lettuce, at the very least. (OK, potato salad. You got me.) The basic salad sandwich usually has lettuce, tomato, cucumber, onion, a little watercress, and sometimes a few slices of boiled egg. If you're fancy, maybe add avocado and rocket (arugula). Depending on preference, you might order cheese, tuna, or ham salad. I know, it's a shocker to have just salad, bare-naked all by itself.

Sausage sandwich: Sausage links in a buttered teacake— brown sauce essential.

Tuna mayonnaise: Tuna salad

The Sandwich Shop/Bakers

Traditional bakers selling sandwiches using their own baked bread are not as easy to find as they once were. Nowadays, they've mostly been replaced by high-street chains. They offer good value for money. Chocolate eclairs, apple cream donuts, cream horns, custard slices, millionaire's shortbread, sausage rolls, and savory pasties are just some of the yummy treats you can find in shops on almost every high street. You'll find no shortage of veggie and vegan options. Vegan sausage rolls became a massive hit when introduced by high-street chain Greggs.

SEVEN

Cheese

When visiting the UK, I make it a priority to eat the cheeses I can't easily find in the US. Britain has hundreds of varieties of cheese. These are some of the most popular.

Caerphilly: A crumbly, light-colored, hard cheese. (W)

Cheddar: Available in depths of flavor, from mild to extra strong. Consider spending a little more for special exclusive versions.

Cheshire: Crumbly, creamy, and perfect on crackers or eaten on its own. The oldest-known recorded British cheese.

Double Gloucester: Smooth golden cheese with a creamy taste.

Lancashire: A creamy cheese similar to Cheshire, though better for toasting.

Red Leicester: A hard, crumbly cheese. It gets its deep red color from vegetable dye. Perfect for cheese on toast.

Stilton: A rich, strong, aged cheese with a rind. Can be with or without blue veins. Added to soups, eaten with crackers, or paired with a glass of Port.

Stinking Bishop: Made famous by the *Wallace and Gromit* films when it was used to revive Wallace. This creamy, distinctive cheese with a pungent aroma is much sought-after. Look for it in specialist cheese shops as you won't find it in regular supermarkets.

Wensleydale: You can find flavors such as Wensleydale with cranberries in supermarkets. If you're visiting the Lake District, pop in to the creamery to experience the full range or check out their website: Wensleydale.co.uk. Wensleydale with apricots, stem ginger, and cheddar with caramelized onions are just a few that had my mouth watering. Oh, and of course, Wensleydale is Claymation figure Wallace's favorite cheese.

French cheeses are also popular and widely available in stores and restaurants in the UK.

I've only touched on a tiny fraction of the cheeses available in the UK. Please don't ask for cheese in a can. We will send you to sit in a corner until your taste buds have returned to normal.

EIGHT

The Sweet Spot

Cakes, Desserts, and Puddings

If you've watched any of the popular baking shows, you'll know that Britain is known for its wonderful cakes and sweet creations. There's been a resurgence in the popularity of traditional puddings. Once scoffed at as being the stodgy fare served up at school dinners, they're now re-created and rebranded as gourmet desserts. This list will help you recognize the items on menus.

Puddings

You will discover below that a British pudding is an entirely different dessert from the creamy custard-style one that Americans may imagine.

Whether you decide to eat your pudding with hot sweet custard, ice cream or fresh (whipped cream) is up to you. However, cream in a can has the same rule as cheese. It's forbidden. Brits call it "squirty cream," but you still can't have any!

Apple/fruit crumble: Cooked with sweetened apples—or maybe blackberries or rhubarb—covered with crumbly, unconstructed pastry.

Banoffee pie: Banana and toffee cheesecake

Chocolate fudge cake: Chocolate cake covered in chocolate fudge icing.

Eton mess: A mash-up of meringue, fruit, and cream.

Eve's pudding: Baked apples with a sponge-cake topping.

Fool: A dessert of pureed fruit

Jam roly-poly: A flat suet pudding spread with jam, rolled up, and baked. Once a mainstay of school dinners.

Pavlova: Australian-inspired fruit- and cream-topped meringue pie.

Rice pudding: This traditional sweet dish can be as simple or fancy as you like. Thankfully, it doesn't have to be the stuff they served you for school dinners that came with skin.

Sherry trifle: Layers of jelly (Jell-O), custard, fruit, and cream, and laced with sherry.

Spotted dick: Traditional steamed pudding with currants. Never under any circumstances refer to it as *dick pudding.*

Sticky toffee pudding: The most fabulous comfort food. As described in the Baking section.

Syllabub: Sweet cream blended with sherry, wine, or lemon juice.

Treacle tart: Pastry filled with sweet and sticky treacle.

British supermarkets have a wonderful collection of baked goods, as well as mouth-watering cream cakes and fresh puddings. If you visit the UK, I highly recommend you spend time in the big supermarket chains and stock up on supplies to bring home. (Check with customs what you may import and declare anything that requires it.)

Biscuits (Cookies)

A cup of tea isn't complete without a biscuit or two. In the UK, we will judge you by the type of biscuits you serve. No one wants to eat the old, soft crumbs at the bottom of the biscuit tin. You have a biscuit tin, right?

There are many options to choose from. I won't be so forward as to suggest the biscuits you should have on hand, though you can never go wrong with Hobnobs and Jaffa Cakes. And if you want to be fancy, a few foil-wrapped biscuit bars among the regular biscuits are sure to set your biscuit game up for success.

British biscuits are less chewy and more crunchy than the ones you are used to in the US. Biscuits are mostly sold in individual sleeve/roll-type packets, but you can also find biscuit tin assortments, especially around Christmas. Let's look at some of the popular varieties.

Bourbon creams: One of the most popular biscuits are chocolate-flavored rectangular biscuits, sandwiched together with chocolate cream.

Caramel wafers: Chewy caramel wafers covered in milk chocolate.

Chocolate teacakes: Chocolate-covered marshmallow with a biscuit base and a jammie middle.

Custard creams: Another classic. Square vanilla biscuit with a cream filling.

Bourbon and custard creams: So entwined are these in the British biscuit psyche that people struggle to decide which ones they like best. A supermarket has recently offered a solution: a half-custard-cream and half-bourbon version they created.

Chocolate fingers: Shortbread fingers wrapped in delicious chocolate. Available in milk, dark, and white chocolate.

Digestive biscuits: Round biscuit similar to graham crackers. Also available covered in chocolate.

Fig rolls: Like American fig bars

Fruit shortcake: A shortcake biscuit baked with currants and sprinkled with sugar.

Ginger nuts: Hard ginger cookies

Hobnobs: Delicious oat biscuits, also available covered in chocolate. Look out for limited-edition versions.

Jaffa Cakes: Sponge, orange jelly, and chocolate. Is it a biscuit or a cake? Though you will find it in the biscuit aisle, they are officially defined as a cake, and they are delicious.

Jammie Dodgers: Shortbread sandwiched together with jam and cream.

Rich tea biscuits: Simple biscuit. An excellent accompaniment to tea.

Viennese whirls: Melt-in-the-mouth confection sandwiched together with jam and cream.

Many biscuits and chocolate bars are also offered as cake bars. New versions appear regularly with specialty versions. Alongside the traditional items, you will find new twists on old favorites. Look for salted caramel and sticky toffee pudding versions of popular biscuits and cake bars.

Cakes

Here are some favorite cakes found in the baked-goods aisle. Freshly baked versions are available in cafes or bakeries.

Angel layer cake: Layers of pink and yellow sponge, sandwiched together with icing.

Bakewell tart: A short crust base, jam middle, and frangipane (almond) sponge, topped with sliced almonds. Bakewell is a town in Derbyshire, where you can still buy the traditional tart.

Battenberg cake: Checkered yellow and pink cake covered in marzipan.

Brandy snaps: Crisp gingerbread lattice, rolled into hollow tubes, sometimes filled with cream. Traditionally sold at funfairs.

Cherry Bakewells: Mini Bakewell tarts covered in icing and topped with a cherry.

Coffee and walnut cake: Sponge cake baked with coffee and walnuts and filled with buttercream.

French fancies: Small square sponge cakes with a cream topping and coated in colored icing.

Chocolate mini rolls: Mini chocolate sponge rolls filled with cream and coated in chocolate.

Madeira cake: Similar to pound cake.

Millionaire's/caramel shortbread: Squares of shortbread topped with caramel and chocolate.

Swiss roll: A rolled sponge cake filled with jam or cream.

Yum yums: A type of twisted cylindrical donut covered in light icing.

Cream Buns/Cakes

These are found in the refrigerated section of the supermarket.

Apple/jam and cream doughnut: Split torpedo-shaped doughnut filled with jam and cream or apple and cream.

Apple turnover: Triangles of sweet puff pastry filled with baked apple and cream.

Bavarian slice: Layered pastry, similar to a custard slice but filled with cream and jam and topped with sticky, sweet icing.

Chocolate eclair: Cylindrical-shaped choux bun filled with fresh cream and coated in chocolate.

Choux buns: Choux pastry filled with cream.

Cream horn: Sweet puff-pastry horn filled with jam and cream.

Cream sponge: Victoria sponge sandwiched together with jam and cream.

Custard/vanilla slice: Layers of sweet pastry with a filling of custard cream.

Elephant's foot: Large choux pastry cake filled with cream and topped with chocolate icing.

Profiteroles: Chocolate-covered, cream-filled mini choux buns. Similar to a cream puff.

Sweets and Chocolate

Once you've explored the biscuits and cakes, it's time to check out British sweets (candy) and chocolate. An array of delicious chocolate delights awaits you. You will find milk, dark, and white chocolate filled with nuts, raisins, truffles, ganache, fruit cream, and peppermint. There are vegan options from many chocolate manufacturers. Again, the value for money is hard to beat. Specialty chocolate shops are a great place to find gifts. You can also find a massive variety in supermarkets, often with special deals. British airports also are a good place to buy chocolate if you don't get all you need before you leave. One thing I can guarantee is that if you take a trip to the UK and bring back chocolate, it will never be too much once you get home. If you are in the UK at Easter, check out the Easter egg range. See the Holiday and Celebrations chapter for more information.

A '99' Ice Cream

The sound of the ice-cream van signals the first sign of summer. Hopefully they will serve a 99, a cone of soft ice cream with a Cadbury's Chocolate Flake inserted and topped with raspberry sauce. Other trimmings include chopped nuts and *hundreds and thousands*—that's sprinkles to you.

British Chocolate Melts Easily

British chocolate is made differently from that in the US. It doesn't have additives to stop it from melting. If you are bringing it to a warm part of the US, it will melt or go soft quickly.

NINE

Holidays, Celebrations, and Traditions

The United Kingdom doesn't have a season known as "the holidays." We don't generally celebrate Thanksgiving—well, we're hardly going to celebrate you leaving us! What you call "vacations," we call "holidays." We call individual holidays "bank" holidays. Here, we'll focus on the holidays or celebrations that feature specific foods.

Bonfire Night/Plot Night

Every year on the 5th of November, the country comes together to celebrate Guy Fawkes's failed 17th-century plot (the Gunpowder Plot of 1605) to blow up the Houses of Parliament. We burn his effigy on bonfires and set off fireworks. Alongside the pyrotechnics are foods that are popularly eaten. As bonfire night falls in the colder months of the year, many of these warm and comforting foods are easily eaten while standing.

Jacket potatoes (baked potatoes)

Once a popular choice for those hosting their own bonfire. The potato would be wrapped in tinfoil and carefully placed at the bonfire's edge to cook. Obviously, there are safety risks with this method, and it's likely fallen out of favor. There also are fewer local bonfires. The tradition has shifted to safer, organized events and family activities at local pubs.

Pie and peas

A warm pork pie with mushy peas and mint sauce is the perfect comfort food to enjoy while warming by the golden glow of a bonfire's embers.

• • •

Plot toffee

This brittle, almost translucent, rich, dark toffee cooked with black treacle is rarely seen outside of the 5th of November.

Soup

A mug of hot soup is a warming choice for Bonfire Night hunger pangs.

Toffee apples

Apples covered in crunchy, sticky toffee are the perfect way to end your Bonfire Night.

Yorkshire parkin

Parkin is a traditional bar cake eaten around Plot Night. It is, as you can guess, a very Northern sweet treat. The ingredients that give it the special flavor and consistency include ginger, treacle, oats, and brown sugar.

Christmas

A traditional Christmas dinner will include some, if not all, of the following.

Roast turkey: The deep-fried variety has yet to become popular.

Brussels sprouts: Another food that has a polarizing effect, especially if you grew up in a household where they were cooked to a mushy pulp. Once I learned it wasn't obligatory to dissolve them over a slow heat before serving, I began to appreciate them.

Cranberry sauce: Eaten with the turkey, and sometimes on Boxing Day with cold leftovers.

Pigs in blankets: Mini sausages wrapped in bacon. Different from the pastry-covered sausage roll type.

Roasted parsnips: Roasted root vegetable

Roast potatoes (roasties): There is nothing quite like oven-roasted potatoes. Sometimes partly boiled first, but always cooked in hot fat and oil, or a combination. Crisp perfection on the outside and fluffy inside. The household may also choose to cook them in duck or goose fat, because they have it from the bird they are cooking, or they might just be fancy.

Stuffing: Seasoning

Turkey gravy: The brown stuff. Often made with fat from the bird, sometimes with the addition of time-saving, store-bought gravy granules or cubes.

Yorkshire pudding: If you are not from Yorkshire, you might not see this, but they're a perfectly acceptable addition to Christmas dinner.

Christmas cake: Rich fruit cake. Traditionally iced with marzipan and royal icing. In Yorkshire we eat it with a slice of cheese.

Christmas pudding: Rich fruit pudding served with brandy sauce or brandy butter. Traditionally a silver coin was baked into the pudding and the lucky recipient was promised future good fortune. Choking hazards and the risk of broken teeth have caused the tradition to wane.

Mince pies: Sweet pastry pies, filled with spiced dried fruit, often infused with alcohol. On the night before Christmas, Brits traditionally leave Santa Claus a mince pie and a glass of sherry or whatever alcohol is on hand. I've heard that milk and cookies are becoming popular. This Americanism must cease immediately if British children expect to get the gifts they hope for.

Mulled wine: Spiced wine served hot.

Yule log: Rolled sponge cake filled with cream and coated in chocolate cream, decorated to look like a festive log.

Boxing Day: The day after Christmas is a widely celebrated holiday. Leftovers are often on the menu, served as a buffet tea. You might see turkey sandwiches, pork pies, Christmas cake, and mince pies.

Easter

The traditional roast eaten at Easter is lamb. You'll also find lots of indulgent options for hot cross buns—yet another excuse to sneak salted caramel into everyday items. Where Brits excel is in the Easter egg department.

Easter Eggs

Visit the UK before Easter and you'll find a massive selection of chocolate Easter eggs. Most chocolate and sweet manufacturers make their own versions, usually including one of their products inside the hollow chocolate egg or in the enclosing box. When you're faced with entire aisles dedicated to every conceivable size and type of chocolate egg, from simple to luxurious, it's difficult to choose between them.

Pancake Tuesday/Shrove Tuesday

The day before Ash Wednesday—a more demure affair than Mardi Gras. On this day, we cook, flip, and eat pancakes. British pancakes are thin, like French crepes, and traditionally served sprinkled with sugar and lemon juice.

The Seaside (The Coast/Ocean)

Before Brits began traveling abroad, holidays often meant visiting towns on the coast. As water surrounds the UK, most people don't have too far to go to find what is affectionally called the *Seaside*. On warm bank holiday weekends, the seaside will be packed with visitors.

Seaside Food

The British seaside has its own food traditions. Expect to find seafood, including cockles, mussels, crabs, winkles, and whelks. You'll also find food you're used to seeing at state fairs in the US. Fish at the seaside is usually fried with the skin on.

Rock

A uniquely British confection, usually only found at the seaside. A stick of rock candy (shortened to "rock") is a hard, cylindrical candy stick—like a thick candy cane. The name of the town or resort is embossed throughout the stick so that wherever it is broken, the name appears. Rock is often peppermint or aniseed flavor, though there are many varieties, styles, and sizes available. It was once a tradition to bring friends and family a gift of a stick of rock after visiting the seaside.

Buffets

What you might find on a buffet in a British home depends on where you are in the United Kingdom and determined by background, income level, and choice. The following items make up a buffet found in many households, whether a birthday tea, a funeral wake, or even a simple wedding.

A buffet for a special occasion held in a hired venue may have fancier fare, including fresh salmon, cuts of meat, and many specialty desserts. I've focused on a basic buffet commonly shared in households across the country.

Traditional

Breadsticks

Cheese and crackers

Cheese and onion quiche

Cheese dip

Cheese straws

Chicken drumsticks

Cocktail sausages

Coleslaw

Crudités and dips: Chopped vegetables for dipping.

Fairy cakes

French bread: Cut diagonally and displayed with a pack of butter and a knife.

Garlic bread

Hummus

Jelly and ice cream

Mini chocolate eclairs

Mixed bowl of unidentifiable crisps

Party rings: Sweet iced biscuits

Pasta salad

Pickled onions

Pizza slices

Pork pies: Cut into quarters

Potato salad

Quiche Lorraine: Open-faced pie with an egg and bacon filling.

Satay sticks: Individual skewers of meat with peanut sauce.

Sausage rolls: Sausages wrapped in pastry.

Scotch eggs: Hard-boiled eggs wrapped in sausage meat, coated in breadcrumbs, and fried.

Falafel, samosas, and bhajis: Supermarket-bought

Tortilla chips and dips

Vol-au-vents: Puff pastry case filled with thick, creamy meat or a fish-based sauce.

Sandwiches

Brits often serve sandwiches with sliced white bread cut into triangles. You may also find sandwich fingers or open sandwiches using half a teacake—not the ones with raisins.

Sandwich Fillings

Beef and onion

Cheese and onion

Coronation chicken: Curried chicken in a sauce.

Egg and cress sandwiches: Egg mayonnaise with a sprinkling of watercress.

Fish paste sandwiches, salmon, or tuna

Ham and mustard

Prawn mayonnaise: Prawns in a Marie Rose sauce.

Roast chicken

Tuna mayonnaise

Old-fashioned Buffet Food

Cheese-and-pineapple or cheese-and-onion porcupine: A popular 1970s buffet centerpiece. Half of a large, round fruit, covered in foil. Add cocktail sticks (toothpicks) with cocktail sausages, pickled onions, and squares of cheese, or cheese and pineapple chunks to resemble a hedgehog.

Cheese balls: Snacks with a crispy outer and cream-cheese filling.

Sliced onions or cucumber in vinegar

Weddings

Weddings in the UK, as in the US, can be as unique (weird?) as the couple getting married.

If you're invited to a wedding, you might attend the main reception, usually held in the afternoon. If you're a second-tier friend, they might invite you to the *night do*. Don't feel slighted; it's often much more fun than the daytime event and without the boring speeches.

Some receptions run all the way through to the evening. You might attend both and stay all day. Daytime receptions are usually either a sit-down meal served by wait staff or a buffet that could still be a hot meal, but served to you as you line up at the buffet table.

Evening wedding events come in all shapes and sizes. They can be creative with quirky themes that represent the couple's tastes. At one "do," I saw guests line up for hot bacon sandwiches made with homemade bread rolls. After a night of drinking and dancing, it was a popular choice. At another, guests were served their choice from dozens of variations of sausages, mashed potatoes, and gravy to make up a unique supper of *bangers and mash*. At the simpler and inexpensive end of the scale, I've seen wedding buffets of the traditional variety, including one in Yorkshire with the unusual addition of black pudding. Another event wowed the crowd with an extensive menu of Indian food, catered from the local restaurant. There is no one traditional wedding banquet. Go hungry and be prepared for anything.

TEN

Tea

Visit a Brit at home and they'll offer you a cup of tea or coffee. We don't limit this to friends and family. If construction workers or installers are visiting a home, they'll rarely get down to work until they've drank at least one cuppa. Affectionately called builder's tea, it usually comes with two sugars, and preferably a biscuit or three.

We've dismissed a few stereotypes about British food, yet what you've heard about our love of tea is likely true. Tea is our national addiction. British children become tea makers as soon as their parents believe they're old enough to safely handle a kettle. They then take turns in making tea with everyone else in the household for the rest of their lives. As a Brit in the US, I'm deeply disappointed that my American husband's attitude toward tea making is to offer to boil the water. Brits understand the social contract. You put the kettle on; you make the tea. I suggest any Brit considering marrying an American first consider a pre-nup for all things tea-related.

If Brits encounter a shock or receive bad news, someone will put the kettle on and make them a cup of tea. When faced with any situation where you aren't sure what to do next, tea is also the answer. If you need to broach a delicate subject, challenge someone, or settle an argument, tea will grease the wheels of the peacemaking process. Brits make tea with boiling water from a kettle—you might know it as a teakettle. Every British home has one. Never make tea in a microwave. If someone asks you to put the kettle on, that means fill with water and turn on the kettle to boil for tea.

Once you've boiled the kettle, make the tea immediately; tea requires boiling water. If there's water left in the kettle, don't re-boil the same water when making another drink later.

Only boil what you need and use fresh water each time for the freshest flavor. For the traditional experience, use a teapot and maybe even proper tea with tea leaves. If you're using tea bags, three is usually enough for an average-size teapot. For extra authenticity, warm the pot first with boiled water. Pour the water out before you add the tea and hot water. After you've made tea, give it a stir, and keep the pot warm with a tea cosy (cozy in the US).

The debate over whether you put the milk or tea in the cup first continues to be hotly debated. The habit of putting milk in first may have come about to avoid the hot tea cracking delicate porcelain or China teacups. Be honest. Are you using a teacup, or are you like most people and drinking it out of a mug? Put your tea in first, otherwise you risk it being too weak. If after you've poured a little tea into the cup and you can see it's not the right color, tip it back into the pot for longer. Weak, wishy-washy tea will not usually be well received. Be careful not to leave the tea bag in the hot water for too long or you'll stew the tea, making it past its best. Squeezing the tea bag against the cup can also spoil the flavor. You may hear the tea-making process referred to as brewing, mashing, or steeping.

For the full British tea experience, we recommend dunking: dipping a biscuit in your tea. You may need to practice finding the optimum point for dunking before the biscuit dissolves and sinks to the bottom of your cup. Explore from the fabulous range of biscuits available to discover which is the most suitable and enjoyable. There are many types of tea, though tea made from black tea leaves is the most commonly consumed.

ELEVEN

Baking and Ingredients

Brits rarely refer to baking as "made from scratch." If you're baking, unless you're using a cake mix, it's almost always made from scratch. Putting aside the theatrical concoctions on baking competitions, traditional baking can be delightfully simple. If you suddenly have an urge for a cake, dessert, or biscuits and have run out of your favorites, you could order them to be delivered, as is becoming popular on both sides of the pond. Or you can make your own in about as much time as it will take to place an order and wait for delivery.

Biscuits (cookies) are quick and easy to make if you have a basic store cupboard. Similarly, a cake can be whipped up quickly. A basic recipe such as a Victoria sponge comprises only four basic ingredients: flour, butter, sugar, and eggs.

You can be as elaborate and fancy as you like once you become more confident. The wonderful thing about baking is that if it is not too burned to be edible, you can still enjoy it. You can slather a too-dry cake in cream or custard, and you can eat a crumbly biscuit with a spoon.

I learned to bake with my mum. There's a magic to eating a cake fresh from the oven, still warm, that you had a hand in making. After waiting impatiently and experiencing the aromas at each stage of the baking process, seeing the finished product is a pleasure I enjoy to this day—from scraping the cake mix into the greased baking tin to carefully opening the door to watch its progress. Baking is a wonderful and fun activity to do with a parent. And who remembers taking a turn to lick the mixing bowl before it was washed?

I've listed the British name for ingredients so you will know what to look for if you do any baking.

Baking Ingredients

Bicarbonate of soda: Baking soda. (Baking powder is baking soda with cream of tartar.)

Black treacle: Thick-and-sticky dark treacle. Used in baking gingerbread. It's similar to, but certainly not the same as, molasses. Hard to find in stores, but available online or in specialty shops.

Bread flour: Strong flour

Caster sugar: Refined sugar

Currants: Used to make Eccles cakes. These are not always easy to find in the US. I have found them in the refrigerated section of health-food stores.

Dates: A vital ingredient if you want to make sticky toffee pudding.

Demerara sugar: Light brown sugar with a crunchy texture.

Desiccated coconut: Shredded coconut

Double cream: Heavy cream

Flaked almonds: Sliced / slivered almonds

Golden syrup: There's no substitute for golden syrup. The thick and sticky consistency is different from other syrups. As it's available in the British section of many stores or online, it's worth making the effort to use it for best results.

Icing sugar: Powdered sugar

Lard: Shortening

Marzipan: Paste of ground almonds

Plain flour: All-purpose flour

Rolled oats: Old-fashioned oats

Sea salt: Kosher salt

Self-raising flour

Strawberry jam: Strawberry preserves or jelly

Sultanas: Golden raisins

Fresh Baker's Yeast

You may occasionally see a recipe that asks for fresh yeast. In the past, fresh yeast, rather than the dried packet variety, was widely used for baking in the UK. It has become harder to find. Supermarkets often sell small packages, or those who bake bread might give away individual amounts on request. I have never seen fresh yeast available in the US or know anyone who has used it.

Kitchen and Cooking Terms

Baking foil: Tinfoil/aluminum foil

Hob: Stove

Sieve: Strainer

Cooker: Oven

Creme pâtisserie: Pastry cream

Baking tray: Baking sheet

Bun tins: Muffin tins

Coulis: Thin sauce, usually sweet. You may have a raspberry coulis drizzled on to your dessert.

Grated: Shredded

Greaseproof paper: Similar to parchment paper but does not contain a nonstick surface, so the tray and paper must be greased for baking use.

Grill: Broil

Proving: Rising

Plait: Braid. Bread twisted into a plait for a decorative effect. Plaits are what Brits call hair braids.

Soggy bottom: Undercooked base of a pie or pastry.

Tray bake: A dessert such as flapjacks that is baked on a baking tray and cut into squares or slices.

Vegan or Vegetarian Substitutions

Many traditional British recipes call for lard (shortening), butter or margarine, and eggs. If you want to create a vegetarian version, replace the lard with butter or margarine. For vegan versions, there are good vegan margarines available on both sides of the pond. I also find that when making tray-bakes such as flapjacks, coconut oil and/or peanut butter work reasonably well. Like most things with baking, it's a matter of trial and error.

Popular and Easy British Recipes

I'm not a professional cook, so I've not included recipes. There are so many wonderful British cookbooks and recipes available that I want you to explore and find what suits you.

These are some popular British treats that you will find recipes for in British recipe books or online.

Butter icing: Icing made with butter and icing sugar.

Butterfly buns: A favorite at children's parties. The top of a cooked bun/fairy cake is sliced off and cut into two pieces. Butter icing is added, and the pieces are arranged to resemble butterfly wings.

Cornflake crispy buns: Easy to make and popular for children's parties. Cornflakes or rice cereal, covered in chocolate.

Fairy cakes: Cupcakes made with a simple glace icing.

Flapjacks: A tray bake made with cornflakes, oats, golden syrup, sugar, butter, and flour. This is one of our household favorites and I amend with whatever breakfast cereal we have on hand.

Fruit crumble: Apple, blackberry, or rhubarb covered in an unconstructed pastry mixture made of flour, butter, and sugar. When the sticky fruit sauce bubbles to the surface, it is ready to be served with custard, cream, or ice cream.

Glace icing: Sugar and water icing, sometimes with added food coloring.

Gingerbread: Traditional rich ginger slab cake.

Gingerbread men: A decorated gingerbread biscuit in the shape of a person.

Lemon drizzle cake: A dense sponge cake infused with lemon syrup and drizzled with a zesty lemon icing.

Pancakes: British pancakes are thinner than those found in the US and are more like French crepes. Made with a simple pouring batter using flour, milk, and eggs.

Shortbread: Simple to make, though you need to be careful to not overcook and allow it to turn brown. Flour, sugar, and butter are all you need for the basic recipe.

Sticky toffee pudding: A classic pudding made with dates.

Victoria sandwich cake/Victoria sponge: This classic cake is made with two round cakes sandwiched together with raspberry jam and fresh or butter cream.

Yorkshire puddings: Perfect with a roast dinner. Yorkshire puddings require Yorkshire pudding tins that are shallower than muffin tins. The batter is the same as that for pancakes.

Pastry

Pastry is about the only food I buy pre-made. Making pastry is not complicated, but it is messy and a little time-consuming. Good-quality short crust or puff pastry is an excellent base for a pie, and if you make the filling, you can count it as homemade.

Choux pastry: For eclairs and profiteroles.

Filo pastry: For baklava, samosas, and dishes that require very thin layers of pastry.

Hot-water crust: A hard pastry used for making savory pies.

Puff pastry: Flaky pastry that's labor intensive to make. Used for sausage rolls, pasties, and apple turnovers.

Short crust pastry: The simplest pastry used in both sweet and savory pies. Perfect for cheese straws, mince pies, jam tarts, and quiche.

Metric and Measurements

There has been a post-Brexit push to bring back the imperial measurement system. Most people are used to the metric system. Many know nothing else.

Fresh items are sold by the kilogram, though you may find some stores still unofficially using the old system.

1 kilogram = 2.2 pounds.

Brits use kitchen "weighing scales" to measure ingredients rather than cups.

• • •

High Altitude

In the US, an adjustment of oven temperature is required when baking at high altitude. Elevation affects the consistency of baked products. The UK doesn't have anywhere high enough to affect baking. Unless you are cooking at the top of a mountain, no adjustments are necessary.

Lost-in-translation alert!

A bun is a cupcake/muffin. If someone asks for a bite of your buns, don't be offended.

TWELVE

Food Shopping

When Brits say they're going shopping, it means any kind of shopping and not just for groceries.

You'll need a *bag for life*—a reusable shopping bag. Those bags you forget and leave in the car are a necessity in the UK. Stores no longer offer free plastic grocery bags. Retailers are legally obligated to charge you for bags, with few exceptions. Bags are *for life*, because if they break, you get them replaced for free.

Trolley (Shopping Cart)

Supermarket trolleys are locked together until you insert a pound coin to unlock them. They do this to prevent theft and cart dumping. Your coin is refunded once you return the cart and chain it back into position. Always keep a pound coin on hand in case you need it.

No Tax Added

The UK doesn't charge additional sales tax. The price you see is what you pay, though it may include Value Added Tax (VAT) on applicable items.

The Yellow Sticker Reduced-price Shelf

If you're a bargain shopper and time it right, you can get incredible deals on marked-down food nearing its sell-by date. Fresh produce, cream cakes, bread, ready meals, packaged salads, and sandwiches—anything with a short date—may be heavily discounted. You can usually spot the items by the yellow sticker on the package. Beware of the ruthless bargain shopper who knows the precise time of the price change. They hover around the reduced-price section, waiting for the employee to appear with their pricing gun. They then swoop in and snatch what they can, putting food in their cart without even glancing at it, only to dump their unwanted items when they've had time to look them over. It can be quite a scrum to navigate this cultural activity.

Why would you want all this reduced stuff, you might ask? Much of the food can be frozen, and a cream cake reduced in price to the equivalent of 50 cents is irresistible. Remember to consider the worker doing the reductions. They don't enjoy being shoved out of the way to let you get the last scotch egg.

Frozen, Tinned, and Packet Foods

Foods that have stood the test of time and that Brits love.

Iconic Frozen Food

Arctic roll: Sponge cake wrapped around an ice cream center.

Black forest gateaux: A popular dinner party item on menus in the 1970s and '80s. Rich layers of chocolate sponge, whipped cream, and cherries. For many it was the first introduction to a fancy dessert. The frozen variety was an acceptable alternative to home baking.

Chicken dippers: Chicken fingers coated in breadcrumbs.

Chicken Kiev/Kyiv: Chicken breast stuffed with garlic butter and coated in breadcrumbs.

Fish fingers: Fish sticks

Microwave chips: Perfect getting-in-from-the-pub food.

Potato croquettes: A fluffy mashed potato interior, coated with a crispy breadcrumb wrapping.

Potato waffles: Lattice-shaped savory potato product.

Yorkshire pudding: I'd like to say a Yorkshire person would never use frozen Yorkshire pudding, but we all get busy. Though not as good as home-baked, they are a satisfactory alternative.

Tinned and Packet Foods that Brits Love

Baked beans: Once seen as a utilitarian food. Beans are healthy and good value. They are available in specialty varieties including curry, cheesy, barbecue, and even with vegetarian sausages added.

Mushy peas: Yes, you can get them in a tin.

Sardines: Small, oily fish sold in cans. Packed in oil, tomato sauce, and also in fancier infusions.

Spaghetti hoops: Hoop-shaped pasta in tomato sauce. Perfect on buttered toast.

Crisps and Snacks

Brits love crisps. You've learned that we even put them in our sandwiches. The crisp aisle of a supermarket is a good place to explore traditional and new flavors. Multipacks of six or twelve packets are often the best deal. Bags in multipacks usually weigh 25 grams, which is less than an ounce and will be scoffed (devoured) in no time. The UK may not have the massive bags you see in the US, though you'll still see larger bags for sharing. It is also worth looking at a store's own brand crisps and snacks. You'll find an array of specialty crisps, cheesy-style puffs, potato sticks, prawn cocktail snacks, bacon rashers, and onion rings.

Popular Crisp Flavors

Beef

Cheese and onion—probably the most popular flavor.

Prawn cocktail

Ready salted

Roast chicken

Salt and vinegar

Smoky bacon

Manufacturers periodically introduce specialty-themed crisps and limited-edition flavors. There are lots of posh flavors you can bring out to impress visitors when you get back home.

THIRTEEN

Food and Related Word List

The food list has common British food names and their American alternative. I've listed the British version first.

Afters: Pudding or dessert

Angel Delight: Instant pudding

Aubergine: Eggplant

Bangers: Sausages

Beans on toast: Beans on buttered toast. I know Americans find the idea weird, but don't knock it until you've tried it.

Beef wellington: Steak coated in pâté, wrapped in pastry, and baked.

Beetroot: Beets

Bevvy: Beer / drink

Bill: Check

Black pudding: Savory pudding made of blood. (This *is* as weird as you think.)

Black treacle: Similar to molasses. (Rich, dark treacle used in toffee and some rich cakes like gingerbread.)

Boil in the bag: Frozen ready meal—cod in butter or parsley sauce, microwaved in the plastic bag or boiled in a pan of water.

Boiled sweets: Hard candy

Braising steak: Chuck steak

Branston Pickle: Brown pickle. Comes in jars with chopped vegetables.

Breadsticks (grissini): Crisp, long, thin breadsticks used for dipping or as appetizers.

Brew: Tea

Broad beans: Fava beans

Brown sauce: Steak-type sauce with a thick consistency.

Bubble and squeak: Fried potatoes and cabbage, usually made from leftovers.

Builder's tea: Strong black tea, usually served with milk and sugar, traditionally drank by tradespeople.

Candy floss: Cotton candy

Caster sugar: Refined sugar used in baking.

Cauliflower cheese: Cauliflower cooked in a cream sauce.

Cep mushrooms: Strong-flavored mushroom

Cheese on toast: Grilled cheese

Cheese straws: Fingers of short crust pastry baked with cheese.

Cheese toastie: Toasted cheese/panini.

Chelsea buns: A baked yeast bun that looks like a cinnamon roll with the addition of sultanas, raisins, or other dried fruit.

Chickpeas: Garbanzo beans

Chicory: Endive

Chips: French fries

Clingfilm: Plastic wrap/Saran Wrap

Clotted cream: Traditional cream served with cream teas. Made by slowly heating full fat milk to form a thick, rich cream.

Cocktail sticks: Toothpicks

Colcannon: Similar to bubble and squeak; sometimes made with kale.

Coriander: Cilantro. Brits refer to both the seed and the leaf as coriander.

Corn flour: Cornstarch

Corn on the cob: Corn

Corned beef hash: Chopped corned beef topped with mashed potatoes.

Cornish Pasty: Semi-circle shaped pastry filled with meat, cheese or vegetables.

Coronation chicken: Cooked chicken in a curried mayonnaise sauce.

Cos lettuce: Romaine lettuce

Courgette: Zucchini

Cream tea: Scones with jam and clotted cream—and a pot of tea.

Crème fraiche: Cultured cream, similar to soured (sour) cream. Often added to desserts or fruit.

Crème pâtisserie: Pastry cream filling for sweet pies.

Crisps: Chips

Crumpets: A breakfast item akin to an English muffin.

Crystallized fruit: Candied fruit

Cumberland sausage: Spicy, long-spiraled sausage made of chopped pork.

Curry: Generic term for Indian/Southeast Asian spicy meal. See Indian food section.

Custard tart/egg custard: Sweet pie with a firm egg custard filling.

Custard: Sweet sauce poured over puddings to create the perfect comfort food.

Cutlery: Silverware

Do/a bit of a do: A social gathering. "We're having a bit of a do on Saturday, can you come?"

Double cream: Heavy cream

Dripping: Rendered animal fat produced during cooking. Once spread on bread, eaten out of necessity because of poverty. It has seen a popular resurgence as diet trends have changed.

Dumplings: Baked dough balls cooked in meat stew.

Dundee cake: Fruitcake topped with almonds. (S)

Eggs with soldiers: Soft-boiled eggs with sliced strips of bread or toast (soldiers).

Eggy bread: French toast

Faggots: Meatballs

Fairy cakes: Cupcakes

Fish fingers: Fish sticks

Fish paste/spread: Sandwich spread sold in small jars. Once part of children's teas/buffets. Popular in salmon, tuna, crab, or meat flavors.

Flageolet beans: Young haricot beans

Flan: Fruit pie

Flask (of tea): A vessel for keeping drinks and sometimes food warm. Where tea-making facilities are unavailable such as a building site, a worker will take their own flask.

Fromage frais: Smooth cream cheese used in cooking or as a topping.

Gammon: Salted and cured ham similar to Virginia ham.

Gherkin: Pickle

Glace cherries: Candied cherries

Golden syrup: Rich treacle; used in cake and biscuit recipes.

Goujons: Deep-fried pieces of fish or chicken.

Gypsy tart: Sweet pastry tart from Kent. Made with a filling of evaporated milk and sugar.

Haggis: Seasoned dish of cow or sheep offal, blended with grains and suet. Traditionally cooked in a bag made from an animal's stomach. (S)

Halloumi: Grilling cheese made from sheep's milk—traditionally from Cyprus. Its meat-like consistency means it cooks without falling apart when grilled.

Hot cross buns: Sweet fruit bread roll, decorated with an iced cross. Eaten during the period leading up to Easter.

Ice pole: Popsicle (S)

Ice pop: Popsicle

Icing sugar: Powdered sugar

Icing: Frosting

Jacket potato: Baked potato

Jam: Jelly

Jellied eels: Chopped eels cooked in a spicy sauce, left to set, and eaten cold. Traditionally eaten in the east end of London.

Jug: Pitcher

Kendal Mint Cake: Peppermint-flavored tablet, popular nutrition for walking or mountaineering. Famously utilized by the team who were the first to successfully climb Mount Everest.

Kippers: Smoked herring

Kitchen paper/kitchen roll: Paper towel

Knickerbocker glory: Ice cream sundae

Lancashire hotpot: Stew topped with sliced potatoes.

Lardy cake: Tea bread made with lard.

Lemon curd: Fruit spread made with eggs. Also called *lemon cheese*.

Malt loaf: A rich, dense, and fruity bread with the consistency of cake and often eaten spread with butter.

Mange tout: Snow peas

Marie Rose sauce: Cocktail seafood sauce used to make prawn cocktail.

Marmite: A love-it-or-hate-it spread made of yeast extract. (A little goes a long way. Try it on toast.)

Marrow: Squash

Melon boat starter: Boat-shaped slice of melon served with rolled-up Parma ham. The starter of choice for dinner parties in the 1970s.

Minced meat/mince: Ground beef. Not to be confused with mincemeat, a sweetened, dried fruit mixture eaten in pies at Christmas.

Mooli (daikon): Large white radish

Mulligatawny soup: A curry-style soup originating from British rule in India.

Neeps and tatties: Mashed swede (rutabaga) and potatoes. (S)

New potatoes: Small young potatoes

Oatcakes: Oat-based snack. A mixture of a cracker and a biscuit. Popular in Scotland.

Pease pudding: A side dish made of yellow split peas; similar to mushy peas. Common to Northumbria.

Piccalilli: Mustard-based pickle/relish of spiced, chopped vegetables.

Pickled eggs: Boiled eggs pickled in seasoned vinegar or brine.

Pickled onions: Bite-size onions pickled in vinegar.

Pie and mash: Minced meat pie and mashed potato, served with a green parsley sauce. Traditional working-class food eaten in London.

Pies: When Brits refer to pies, they almost always mean the savoury (savory) variety.

Pigs in blankets: Small chipolata sausages wrapped in bacon. Popular at Christmas.

Pilchards: Small herring-type fish, sold in cans. A larger more, mature version of sardines.

Pips: Seeds

Plain flour: All-purpose flour

Ploughman's lunch: See Pubs.

Polony: Similar to bologna

Pop: Soda

Pork pie: Savory pie made with a hot-water crust filled with processed pork and topped with meat jelly.

Pork scratchings: Pork rinds

Porridge: Oatmeal

Potted meat/potted beef: A traditional sandwich spread, usually available from a butcher's shop.

Made of ground-up meat topped with a layer of fat.

Prawn cocktail: Small prawns in a Marie Rose cocktail sauce, served cold as an appetizer. British cocktail sauce is like Thousand Island dressing.

Prawn: Shrimp

Queen of puddings: Custard-type pudding topped with jam and meringue.

Rocket: Arugula

Rolled oats: Old-fashioned oats

Runner beans: Green beans

Saffron cake: Traditional golden spiced cake from Cornwall.

Salad cream: A very British condiment. More frequently used in sandwiches than salads; tastes a little like mayonnaise with the consistency of ranch dressing.

Sardines: A young pilchard; herring-type fish.

Sausage rolls: Sections of sausage links baked in puff pastry.

Saveloy: Spicy sausage sold in fish-and-chip shops.

Scampi: Fried shrimp in breadcrumbs.

Scones: Like American biscuits but sweeter. Served with jam and cream or butter.

Scotch broth: Traditional Scottish soup made with meat, barley, and vegetables.

Scotch eggs: Hard-boiled eggs, wrapped in sausage meat, coated in breadcrumbs, and fried.

Scouse: Meat and vegetable stew popular in Liverpool.

Semi-skimmed milk: Low-fat milk

Semolina: Cream of wheat

Sherbet: Powdered candy for dipping.

Single cream: Pouring cream. The closest US alternative is half and half.

Skimmed milk: Nonfat milk

Smarties: Sugar-coated chocolate candies. Different than the US candy.

Sorbet: Sherbet

Sorrel: Wild salad plant with a tart flavor.

Soured cream: Sour cream

Sponge fingers: Thin sponge-type confection with rounded ends used in desserts and as a base for trifle.

Spring onions: Green onions/scallions

Squash/cordial: Sweet fruit concentrate. Made to be diluted with water. A children's drink or a mixer with alcohol.

Stew and dumplings: Meat and vegetable stew with suet dumplings cooked in the stew.

Sussex pond pudding: Heavy lemon- or apple-filled suet pudding.

Sultanas: Golden raisins

Supernoodles: Similar to Ramen noodles

Swede: Rutabaga

Tablet: Fudge-type confection. (S)

Takeout: Takeaway

Tart: Open-face pie

Tea towel: Kitchen towel

Toad in the hole: Sausages baked into Yorkshire pudding.

Toffee apple: Candy apple

Tripe: Cow's stomach lining

Turkey crown: The top part of a turkey. Sold in supermarkets at Christmas. Marketed to those who don't want to cook an enormous bird and have leftovers for the next month.

Vol-au-vents: Puff-pastry case filled with thick meat- or fish-based creamy sauce.

Water biscuits: Crackers for cheese. Don't dunk these in your tea.

Welsh rarebit: A thick, rich cheese topping made with spices and beer. Served over toast.

Wholemeal: Whole wheat

Worcestershire sauce: Spicy sauce. Used in cooking and added to a Bloody Mary. Pronounced "Wuster."

Yorkshire pudding: A savory accompaniment to a roast dinner. See Pub section.

Food Sayings and Slang

A different kettle of fish: Saying something that is irrelevant to the conversation or related to a completely different set of circumstances.

Cheesed off: Annoyed or irritated

Finger in every pie: Involved in many businesses, projects, or activities.

Full of beans: Energetic

My stomach thinks my throat's been cut: I'm extremely hungry.

On the breadline: Living in poverty

Over egg the pudding: To exaggerate a story

Pea souper: Old-fashioned term referring to fog.

Shut yer cakehole: Shut up

Sure as eggs are eggs: The certainty that something will happen.

To butter someone up: To compliment someone or be extra nice to them to gain favor.

Take the biscuit: Take the cake; to do something shockingly annoying.

Your eyes are bigger than your belly: Said when someone orders too much food or piles their plate and cannot finish it.

Thank You for Reading

I hope you've enjoyed learning about the food of the United Kingdom. Though this is only a brief guide, I'm excited for you to use it as a starting point to discover some of the wonderful food that awaits you.

Acknowledgements

Reading Team/Fact Checkers

Thanks to the invaluable team of readers who are so generous with their time.

Paula Cusack

Peter Cusack

Teresa Jack

Bethany Lingard

Jennifer Reeves

About the Author

Trish Taylor was living and working in England, happily settled in her 14-year role as a career counselor and part-time jazz singer. An encounter with a Salsa-dancing American literally swept her off her feet. They married and moved to the United States. She now writes and speaks.

Connect at www.trishtaylorauthor.com.

Also by Trish Taylor

Put the Kettle On: An American's Guide to British Slang, Telly and Tea

Fiction

A Thousand Reasons Not to Run

Self-help/Business

Yes! You Are Good Enough: End Imposter Syndrome, Overthinking and Perfectionism and Live the Life YOU Want

I'm Never Drinking Again: Maybe It's Time to Think About Your Drinking?

Co-author of *Respect in the Workplace: You Have to Give It to Get It*

Printed in Great Britain
by Amazon

86919492R00079